Things We Can't Escape

Poetry for the Brokenhearted

Diana Townsend

Things We Can't Escape:
Poetry for the Brokenhearted

Copyright © 2023 Diana Townsend
All images are provided and licensed for use by
Canva.com.
Credit for Interior Images: victoria-rusyn
All rights reserved.

DEDICATION

I dedicate this book to anyone
who has ever suffered from a
broken heart,
gone to work with a broken heart,
lost sleep because of a broken heart,
and those who had to learn the hard way
that heartbreak does not come with
an expiration date.

xoxo

Trigger Warning:

This book of poetry is about grief, love, and healing. There are possible triggers and as an author, I do not want to cause anyone unnecessary suffering. Some of the poetry will include thoughts of suicide, depression, acts of suicide, pregnancy loss, natural death, physical and/or emotional abuse, and just an overall sense of sadness within each poem. I want readers to enjoy this work and be prepared for the topics that will arise... I hope this warning page helps and I wish you all love and light.

Diana Townsend xoxo

TABLE OF

CONTENTS

ACKNOWLEDGMENTS

I would like to take this time and thank my family and friends who bought and read my first book. I would also like to sincerely thank readers who have supported me with my other books... I hope you enjoyed reading my work and I hope it brought something meaningful to your life. Thank you. Your support means the world to me.
I would like to thank my daughter, Amaya, for her advice on my covers and titles, and my youngest sister, Ciara, for buying and reading my book as soon as it was released. To my husband, Mike, thank you for loving me and cheering me on when I wanted to give up on this process. To my sister, Kristen... I'd give anything to have you here. There's so much I need to tell you... xoxo

Part One: Grief

My father
was only nineteen years old
when he killed himself.

I was an infant
still learning his voice.

I remember,
growing up,
and
wishing I could have
been enough
to keep him here.

When I turned nineteen,
I thought wow,
I've lived longer
than the man who gave me life.

And then I crumbled inside.

Grief hurts
because it reminds us
of words unspoken
plans that were never made
and
everything we dared
take for granted
because we thought
we had more time...

We mourn in different ways
but our hearts
cannot function
under duress
for very long.

It simply wasn't made for that.

To keep beating after such brutal losses.

It seems unfair
that time heals
but it also steals
the memory of your voice
your face
your smile
and your embrace.

The best part of social media
is seeing friends and family
reconnecting
enjoying memories
sharing memes
tagging each other
in silly comment sections...

The worst part
is when a loved one's page
becomes
a memorial.

Infertility
a silent heartbreaker
we tried everything
even bought baby clothes,
as a sign of faith,
for another baby
that never came...

I gave those little clothes
to a donation center
and I remember crying in the
car...
sobs that made my lungs ache

and I resolved
to never hope
or wish
for anything
ever
again.

Telling me to pray about it
when my tears are overflowing
is a slap in the face.

Not because I don't believe
but because I have yet to see
the joy that comes
the morning
after I've lost someone
I loved.

Sometimes you miss someone
who hurt you
and isn't that the
most curious thing?

Their absence leaves a void
closure you'll never receive
invalidation
of pain
you strive to forget.

I saw a beautiful tiny pink casket once
shiny the bright pastel
clashed with the rainy weather
and I kept thinking
it looked like it could fit a baby doll...

it haunted me in my dreams
for awhile
that little life it held
so incomplete
I couldn't process the idea
of how much strength it took
to say goodbye
to her.

My heart breaks for those
who had slow deaths
and in those final moments
were longing
for someone
to hold their hand
until the end.

Fingertips gently breaking water
the ripples of love
disturbed...

he holds her face
like a delicate gem
and watches
and she drifts away
for the last time.

I hope when it's my time
that the memory of me will be
authentic smiles
iced coffee in hand
as I discuss my favorite things,
shopping for expensive hardcovers...

I hope they remember the softness of my hands
that I was all bark and no bite
unless severely provoked,
remember that I did try to be a good person
most times...

that my love was unconditional
but tough all the same
that I named my daughter
after a reality show star
that I was as goofy
as I was depressed...

I could say I miss you
this slow dull ache
in my heart
that makes me cry spontaneously
without trigger or warning
says so much more...

I would trade everything I've gained
to have you back
if you'd be happier here
than wherever
you are
right now.

I just need a few moments
to hear your voice
and just be able to say I love you
one last time
since I assumed I'd have time to tell you
before we found out
you never made it home.

Continued...

I hope
they remember the times
I made them laugh until they cried...

but,
mostly I hope they reminisce
and think
that maybe
it wasn't all so bad,
having me here,
after all...

it wasn't so bad,
having
me
here,
after all...

You are on my mind daily
but every now and then
my mind wanders to the trucker
who hit your car
and I vaguely remember
seeing his tears when he was interviewed on
the news
and feeling a rage I can't describe
and pity

I wonder does he see you in his dreams
shocked awake by the memory
of the life, he snatched away
from so many of us
who adored you
and needed more time with you.

the shrill ring of a telephone
the quiet hello
a fatigued nurse informs you that
he is gone
and you go numb

he wasn't the best father
his quiet demeanor
considered distant
but he would slip a penny
behind your ear
and laugh as you acted
surprised every time
craving more time with him
until his beeper went off
calling him back to work

a long deep sigh
the dreadful work must begin
of burying
a man you loved
but never really understood.

i'm not ready to leave you
don't cry- just listen
there's not much longer
not enough time

i'm not ready to leave you
but there's no choice
this world
was too callous
for my soft spirit
i stopped fighting
but that never meant
i was ready to leave you

promise me
you will go on without me
love again
live again
be true to yourself
now that you no longer
must burden yourself
with my care

Missing you
is
marshmallows in hot cocoa
fuzzy sweaters
Christmas lights and twinkling stars
sappy movies that bring
unexpected tears to my eyes
fresh flowers
soft hugs when I need it the most

I miss you to the point
where my heart
threatens to explode
from the pain.

I held my heart in my hands
and offered it to the gods
in exchange for you
to come back to me...
but they rejected
my empty vessel
and now I live miserably
waiting to see you again.

Nighttime is the worst
my thoughts and dreams
run together
a never-ending marathon
of chaos and destruction
and you...
lost in the flames
forever.

Shattered glass in my heart
melancholy
dull moments of life
spent missing memories
that fade with age
this life is temporary
but
I thought we would
have longer
together.

You left me here
salty tears and blank stares
people sending love and light
not knowing that you were
my shining glory
my temple of hope...
my one true love.

Come back to me, my love...
Or I may soon join you
in the eternal darkness
that you now call home.

Dare I say
that God did not need
another angel...
how many is enough?

We needed you here,
instead.

I have found
that the ugliness of a family
is revealed
when the main matriarch
passes away...
Most grandmothers
are the only thread
holding a family together...

Minc definitely was.

Hey little sister,
mom hasn't been well
since you've been gone...
and while we are here,
I think it's a constant reminder
you are no longer are...

We miss you.

Disassociating
helps a little
the tiny escape from
remembering your last days
quick smiles
the warmth of your tender hug
thoughtful words we'd exchanged...

the escape from the sharp breath
as we identified your body
the sting of the tears
the crisp air that made me
pull my jacket
closer...

I don't ever want to forget
but damn,
it hurts
to remember.

My daughter was two
when you were taken from us
and now she's sixteen
and I wonder...

how did I manage
to go on
this many days
weeks
and years...

without you.

Abandonment
is a different kind of death
for the person is still walking this earth
but has killed the human connection
that binds us together...
how do we mourn
a living, breathing,
reminder
of what could have been
but never was?

How many of us
roam the world
watching horrible people
do terrible things
and question
why our good person is dead
but the monsters are still here
terrorizing innocent souls…?

Pregnancy is an experience
that is hard to explain
but losing a baby...
this I can explain
in detail
for it is the visceral separation
of two souls who were bound together
by love
and the split seeps
the wounds never heal
and the heartbreak
is more than
any one person
should ever have
to bear.

When children bury their parents
there is a sense of foreboding
for who will guide us now
as we wander the world
grown orphans
looking for
our version
of Neverland.

I get weary of this world
and I ponder the notion
of finding sweet release
in falling asleep
never to awake again...
but the guilt
of hurting those
I'd leave behind
keeps me here,
bound tight
and shackled to life
sometimes,
against my will.

I hold you in my heart
a still shot of innocence
and life gone too soon...

I protect the memories fiercely
for if my mind
was to ever forget
my soul would remind me...

I hope you're proud of me
down here trying at this thing called life
without you...

things don't seem the same
flavors aren't as sharp
sunny days seem hazy
and I forget how to have fun...

but I'm here...
and I need to believe that you're watching
and smiling at my fumbled attempts.

You slipped away quietly
the small gasp of breath
unnoticed in my slumber
and I will always feel guilty
for not keeping a more diligent watch
but I sincerely thought
we had more
time...

Believe it or not
I didn't cry
at your funeral...
the tears came later
much later,
and they burned like lava
as they poured down my face...
they burned a hole
in the picture of us
that I kept on my pillow
and I thought I heard
your voice call out a warning
for me
to not get consumed by
the flames.

Every time
we convince ourselves
we are desensitized to violence
the world sends its best demons
to remind us
how to feel.

I was 18 when September 11 happened
and I remember the eerie silence
in my dorm lobby
as I ran downstairs to get cereal and milk...
and the big screen displayed the plane
entering the building
and we stood in awe...
in shock...
in disbelief...
a fever dream.

I cry when I listen to the phone calls
the voicemails people left
as they accepted their fates...

This was my first world event
where I cried for strangers
and feared the unknown.

I didn't fly again until I was 34.

They called and told me
you were not yourself
barely remembered faces
and names...

and I was scared to visit
because I couldn't bear
if you saw me
and asked
"who is she?"

it was selfish of me
to stay away...

and now you're gone.

I miss you so much
sometimes the pain chokes me
and I have to scream into my pillow
to get it all out.

My patience with living
has been trimmed short
because without you
what life is there left
for me to live.

They say life is short
but it feels long to us
who remain behind
living in grief like
wounded
whipped dogs
with broken-hearts...
mourning the ones
who were called home
early

I write you letters sometimes...
and then burn them
and watch the ashes fall
and whisk away into the wind...

I would give anything
to hear your voice
again.

A man once told me
softly and quietly
with dry eyes
that peace does not come in the morning
but it comes in the dead of the night
when the souls transcend
into the quiet hour...

he said that in those moments
we jump up, out of our sleep
thinking we had a nightmare
but unaware
that another life
has slipped through the cracks
of reality.

Mothers shouldn't have to bury their
children...
but the world has mysterious ways
of testing our grief
and pushing us to the very limits
of
sanity.

Grief changed me
and now people think I am cold
because I shut down in the face
of trauma.

My mind has reached it's limit
for the pain it can tolerate
and my heart
is all cried out.

No one explains
that when a loved one dies
their things become public domain
photographs get moved around and taken
jewelry is passed out and relished
and the intimacy of the items
is ruined
forever.

Nothing is scarier to me now
than not speaking my mind
and saying I love you
while I can...
those unspoken words
sting right in the heart
when you need to say them
and it's too late.

Sometimes I wish
I believed in ghosts
just so I could sit with you
and chat
for awhile...

I just want to know
that you're okay
wherever you are
now.

Death brings some closer to God
but it turned me away
and I fell from grace
desperate for the joy
they say comes
in the morning.

It took the phone company
six months
before they reassigned
your phone number...

I know because I continued to call
and listen to your voicemail
knowing you would never
call me back
again.

We had so many plans
and we discussed the future
as if it was ours for the taking
because in youth
the days feel guaranteed
and time feels
infinite.

Is it so very horrible
that sometimes
I wish it had been me?

Peace to all
who lie awake
rocking back and forth
crying and screaming
and asking God why...

I wish us all peace
in these dark hours
when the grief is too much to bear
and the night feels never-ending
and your soul is hollow
because you're missing someone
who once made
you feel
whole.

Part Two: Love

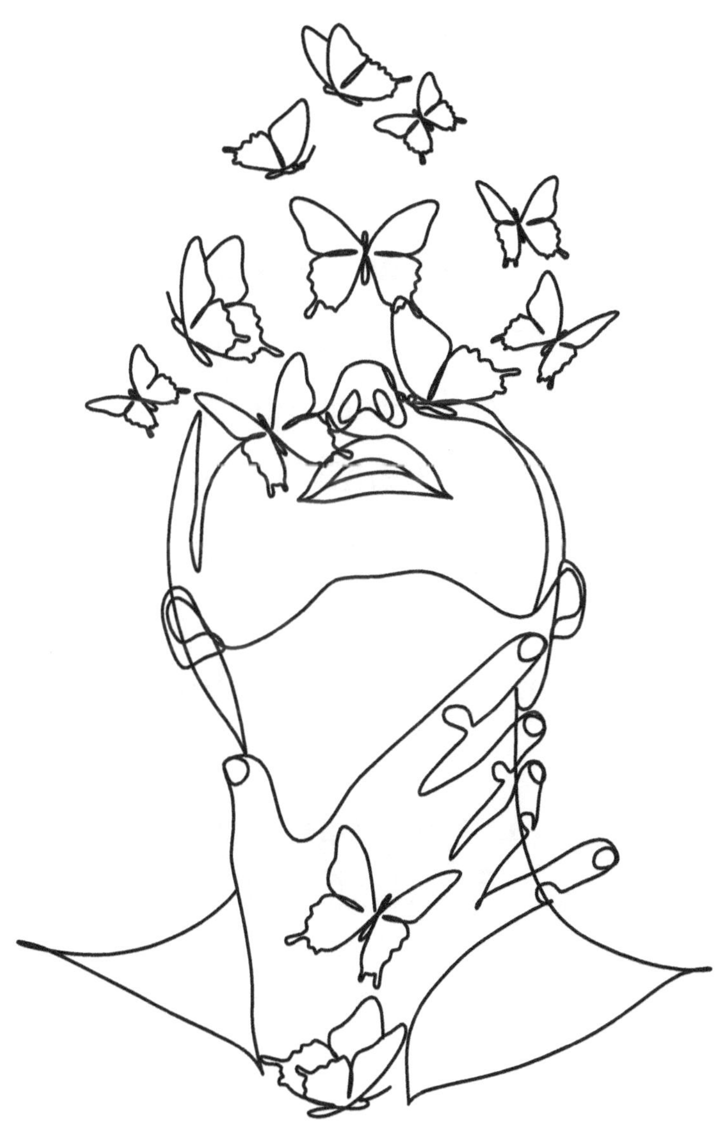

When I think of you
which is far too often
my heart
cracks at the seams
arteries clogged with
pain and regret
thick and heavy
weighing me down...

for I never meant to hurt you
yet
my apologies fell
on deaf ears.

When I hear your voice
I blush and the heat rises to my cheeks
and rushes down to my chest
and I feel alive...

Once we separated
your voice became
a trigger
and I now feel the flush
of anger and the heat
of frustration...

It can all change so quickly...

Our love was
tangled blankets,
arms numb
from the weight of
each other,
a sexy madness
that felt confusing and wild...

and sent me spiraling
once you took it away.

Love does not
leave bruises
tender strikes of flesh
flushed and heated...

"You make me do this,"
is what you told me...

And your anger made me feel guilt
that reminded me of my childhood
and I had to relive
that shameful disappointment
all over again.

The moment our love ended
the ground shivered beneath my feet
and there was an echo
ringing in my ear
of our last goodbye
and as we hugged,
I prayed
that you wouldn't let go
first.

But you did.

Kisses
are temporary stamps
of a love
I think of fondly
while my
weary eyes
weep.

My friends give me a hard time
for missing you the way that I do
shedding tears at brunch
discreetly checking my phone to see
if maybe you had a change of heart
wishing and hoping
that we might run into each other
while I run my daily errands...

Maybe I am overreacting
but I just can't shake
the idea that you were
my forever person.

Were we ever
couple goals?

Our pretty pictures
told a tall tale
that hid the villain
from the world...

He never truly loved her
but she was easy to mold
and so happy to please...
he tolerated her until
he found who he truly wanted
and her discarded heart
became old news
as he moved on to bigger and better things
and she dissolved into
the wind.

He will never think of her again
but she will always remember him
as her first heartbreak.

Weeping willows
never haunted me
until I wept so much
that I considered
hanging low
like those weary branches...

then I knew
that love
had me in a
chokehold.

Sometimes when we snuggled
you would kiss my forehead
and call me baby
and I would smile into your shadow
safe and secure...

I needed that.

I need that back.

What would it take
for us to give this
another chance?

Your mom thought
we were a good fit
and I remember when she told me
I bring out the best in you...

Did you believe her?

I did.

Unfortunately
I loved the potential in you
and my heart
could not see past
my hope for the person I thought you'd
grow into
versus
the person you
truly were
the whole time.

We should be intrigued
by the notion of soul mates
because of seven billion people
how are we all struggling
to find just one
to love
for eternity?

It's fascinating
how
your hoodies still smell
of you
after all
this
time.

Maybe...
it's as simple as this:
you were unworthy
of my unadulterated love
but I gave it anyway,
recklessly,
and I suffered alone
in the aftermath.

I text you
late at night
hoping that one day
it will say
delivered.

The sad thing is...
I would choose you
every single time
in every single situation...

and I would always be
your second choice.

Would you believe me
if I explained to you
that I loved you
after our first conversation?

If I insisted
that my soul had met its mate
the first time my eyes
gazed into yours...

would you believe me?

Logic tells me
that you never truly
belonged to me
but my heart argues
that our souls intertwined
and the heavens sent shooting stars
declaring that I was yours
and you were mine...

so, why did you leave?

We both know
our hearts were not in it...
anymore.

Not after what you did,
what I saw,
the texts I read,
and the lies you told...

And yet, when we finally said goodbye
I cried as if you had died
in my arms.

You kept the little loves notes
I wrote to you
when I was still
just a silly girl...

they remind you
of a time
when I didn't know
any better.

Please do not lie to me
anymore...
I know it's over
and while I wish
it could be any other way...
I am exhausted and drained
from trying to save you
from
yourself.

You should wake up to kisses
on your lips
soft as feathers
and
little notes in your lunchbox
as you prepare to eat
in the breakroom
and
small pats on your back
as you fall asleep
oblivious to the world's problems
for a few hours...

and if you let me
I would give you all of this
and more.

I remember that you took
your coffee black
and your steak well-done
and my love
for granted
and now...

the distance between us is far too wide
to bear.

I was doing okay
scanning each item with
meticulous dedication
whispering hello to customers
and bagging each item with care...
until this elderly gentleman
placed his hand on mine
and said,
"Dear, are you okay?"

and the contact
the sincerity in his voice
the warmth of his hand
broke me
and I sobbed into my hands
because it all
made me think
of you.

It comes in waves
late at night
when the house goes quiet
and begins to settle into itself
and I bundle my blankets
and fluff my pillows
and glance at the empty side of the bed
where you used to
lay.

One day
we will tell the story
of how we met
and we will laugh and crack jokes
and deep down
I will thank the universe
for allowing me time
to love
a beautiful soul
like yours.

Remember how we used to play
and joke about what we would do
if one person ever wanted to
leave the relationship...?

We said we would beg
and plead
and play sad songs on our knees...

When the end came...
we did none of these things
and our anger made us forget
that we were ever
best friends.

The moment
you decided to leave me and our unborn child
you made peace with an idea
that was so horrible...

I remember staring at you in wonder
at how I could have ever loved
someone so empty.

There has to be
a slight trauma
that occurs
when you lose your person
because the relationship goes from
soulmates to strangers
and what could be less
traumatic
than that?

You had a bad habit
of tracing the bridge of my nose
and pinching it between your fingertips...

I wonder if you do that
to her.

I fell in love
with a narcissist
on a sunny day
with dreams in my eyes
and hope for
a soft life.

It was a dream...
deferred.

The moment I filed for divorce
I heard the mocking voice of my aunt,
the accusations of our children,
the pity in my mother's calls...

and I turned it all off
and did what needed
to be done
so that I could have a chance to live
outside of the box
you so carefully
placed me
in.

I thought I loved
the girl I was
when I was with you...

I learned,
that I loved
the girl you wanted me to be
until you left
and I was exposed
as a fraud.

Do I still love you?

I don't really know...
I know my pillows still carry your scent
and I refuse to wash them...
I know my heart skips a beat when
my phone dings...
I know that I cry before work because
we used to carpool and now I drive
alone...

No, I don't think I love you anymore...

And if I say it enough,
maybe I can
convince myself.

He chose her
while he was with me...
and I chose him,
still.

I loved a boy
when I was 12
but my ideas of love
were wrapped in bows
of toxicity and abuse...

I gave him all of me
before I knew
my own worth.

Remembering us
hurts to the point
where I wish
for
nothingness...
I no longer care
to see
to hear
to know
to be aware
or to be
here
without you.

I am often the one
who has to text first
call first
email first
and I know people enjoy me
but I never truly feel
loved
by anyone.

We both know it's over
and it hurts to admit
because I once believed that the stars
aligned to bring us together
that the moon shone down on us
that we were the chosen ones
angels who walked the earth
the personification of true love...
but we haven't weathered the storm
very well
and it's become toxic for me
and I find myself walking on eggshells
to please you and keep the peace...

It's time for me
to pack my bags and my last tidbits
of self-dignity
and find a new
home.

In my final days
I swear to you
I will close my eyes
and release my spirit
so I can find you
in every possible realm
and every possible lifetime.

She knew it was over
when the space between them
became a safe haven of peace
because the interactions between them
were drowned in regret and contempt.

I cheapened myself
and lowered my worth
so you would love me freely...
because high-maintenance girls
are too much work, you told me...
I was willing to accept bae minimum
to be your girl
and I will never forget
begging for love and affection
from a man who
never truly understood
how to love.

There were nights
when I craved you
as one craves a drug...
you were heroin
coursing through my veins
and my intervention
the sudden awakening
that you were no good for me
almost came
too late.

Once,
I heard someone say
while on the train,
"there's no harm in goodbye"
and I thought about you...
and my heart almost exploded
from the sheer misery
of missing you
and I wanted to say,
"Oh yes... yes there is much harm in saying
goodbye."

But I stayed silent
and wiped the tears from
my eyes
and waited on
my stop.

Spending the holidays
alone
isn't what hurts...

Spending the holidays
without the person
who was the love of your life
your forever person...

that's what
hurts.

Oh, I know she was prettier
than I
but I thought
you cared more
for what was inside...

I was wrong.

You taught me
how beautiful it could be
to be selfless...
and for the first time in my life
I focused on making someone else smile
and it was the most
exhilarating experience
of my life.

Part 3: Healing

I guess we all have a moment
where we laugh for the first time
after the event
and forget that we are supposed
to be grieving...

This is the first step.

None of us asked to be here
and yet here we are
trying to navigate this world
and endure it's constant war
against love and goodwill...

keep going.

I heard our song
and it didn't bring to tears
this time...

I smiled and thought of you
and then went back to singing
and laughing with my friends
as we drove
along the highway
with the sun beaming on my face...

Peace comes in pockets
interruptions
in the monotone
motions
of daily life
when I can take a deep breath
and let it all go...

Be kind to yourself
as you go along this journey
for healing takes time
and grief doesn't
expire.

Take small moments
to breathe in
positivity and light
hold it
hold it
hold it
now...
exhale
and release the negativity
the self-doubt
and the self-hate...

repeat as needed.

In the long dark days
it can be hard to remember
that there is light
way up ahead...
run if you can,
and walk if you must,
crawl if necessary...

but please get there.

I smelled his scent today
and it smelled like
lavender and broken dreams
but I inhaled it in,
deep past my heart and into
my core,
and I released it back
to the stars,
and let it go...

Nobody said it would be easy
but why do some people
have it so hard
and how do we muster
the strength to find
beauty
in all of this pain?

I suppose that is what
makes us human...
we learn to smile again
and it lights up
the world.

Healing is
taking those tiny steps
towards living the life
you were meant to live
while nurturing your battle wounds
from surviving the hell
that we call life.

We may find strength
in odd things
and that's okay...

Only you can say
what your journey will look like
to become whole again.

Never feel the need
to justify your healing
to the world.

Some days
washing my face
taking a shower
going to work
spending time with family and friends...

these tasks are a win
because my depression tells me
to stay in bed, call in, and sleep.

Celebrate the small wins.

Sunshine is my favorite
antidepressant.
There's something lovely
about the rays hitting my face
after days spent
stressed at work
or
when I've isolated myself in my home...

Give me sunshine,
give me music,
and I'll make the most
of this thing
called life.

You have to stay hydrated
take your meds
and get enough sleep...
this is common knowledge
but no one prepares you
for the days when
those simple tasks
feel like moving mountains...

Take it a step at a time.

There is still beauty
out there...
Sometimes I have to use
a microscopic lens
to find it
but
I manage.

I'm too afraid
of what I would become
if I couldn't.

Freedom is
allowing yourself to grieve
and feel
and cry as you need to
without the pressure to smile
to make others feel
comfortable.

You have permission
to let it go
whenever you're ready...

release it,
burn it,
hit it,
pound it,
crumble it up...

and let it go.

When we become whole
it means we found the missing pieces
that we lost along the way...

some will be warped,
damaged,
sharper than before...

and that's okay.

Put yourself back together the
best way you can.

There is healing
in the sky
in the flowers
in the trees
in our pets
and friends...
and maybe even in our families.

You will blossom in the safe spaces
you create
in the nucleus
of your world.

Years and decades
do not define
our grief.

You are allowed to cry
whenever the need calls to you
and you are allowed
to feel the sadness
of lost
no matter how long it has been.

It takes courage
to believe in love
after learning
how this world
operates.

Times does not necessarily
heal all wounds
but it does work a certain magic
in creating a distance
between the sorrows of yesterday
and the hope for a better tomorrow.

Please allow yourself
the chance to rest
because you can't save anyone else
while you're on the brink
of losing
yourself.

Life has a way
of showing us the worst days
so we can appreciate
the good ones.

This journey is
a three hundred and sixty five day
climb...

Give yourself credit for each day
you survived...

even if it was
a struggle.

One day you will look back
in awe
because you will remember
what you were up against...
and see that
you still made it.

You're still here.

To the woman I am today:

I am so sorry I deserted you…
and I promise to come back to you,
to be proud of you,
to love you wholly,
to remember the most
beautiful aspects of you,
and I will never sacrifice you
to please someone else…
ever again.

I pray you can learn to trust me again.

There's a chance that
where you are in life now
isn't about finding love
or making other people happy...
no, maybe this road
will lead you to a place
where you're not judged,
you're not pressured to be anything that
goes against your morals,
you are not bound to anyone's
expectations...
You are not defined by other people's
opinions and judgments,
but you are free to finally
love yourself
the way you have so selflessly loved
everyone
else.

Grief does not come
with an expiration date.

We can remain spoiled
and bitter
for as long as we need to.

We lost someone or something
who meant the world to us...

give us time
to heal.

It is okay to grow alone...
we tend to be hesitant
to clear the overgrown weeds
in our gardens
and the beauty
of our new growth
is hidden behind the relationships
that we have long
outgrown.

Don't be too hard on
the version of you
who loved blindly
and was hurt in the process...
don't call yourself dumb
and make jokes about your innocence
for that girl
loved people with her entire heart
and believed that others would offer
their best selves
in return...

and that,
is beautiful.

Isn't it dreadful
that we have been convinced
to think less of ourselves
for being single
as if we were a criminal
or just a truly bad person...

Being alone is not a judgment
or reflection
of your
self-worth.

There is solace
in quiet
for I have learned that
talking too much
about anything at all
never ends well...

I find peace
in not
speaking
about anything
at all.

You deserve
justice and closure
but the world
doesn't always give us
what is rightfully
ours.

Promise yourself
to always make an effort
to treat yourself
the way
you wish
they would
treat you.

Their bad behavior
is definitely
a pattern...

Our willingness to return
to the bad behavior
is also a pattern...

We teach people
how to treat us
by what we decide
to tolerate.

Buy yourself fresh flowers
every week
if you can...

it doesn't solve anything
but they are pretty
and they might
make you smile
and remember the softness
of life.

Be fierce
when protecting your space
guard your heart
and be ready to attack
anyone
who threatens
your peace
of mind.

Sometimes
venting
is the problem...

Write it down
and keep it
or burn it
but
remember that temporary anger
can lead to permanent judgement.

Bloom into
the person you needed
when you were little
or when you felt
the most
unprotected.

Delete old contacts
erase the pictures
that trigger you
or make your cringe
and clean up your friend's list...

you are no longer obligated
to keep connections
with people
who have burned
their side
of the bridge.

Cheer yourself on
even when the silence
from your family and friends
is deafening.

Healing exposes the best
and worst
parts of who we are,
who we have loved,
and who we wish we could
be.

About the Author

Diana Townsend is a mom to a really cool teenager, a wife to a somewhat cool husband, and an educator at heart. She loves to write poetry, read women's fiction, and watch movies with strong female leads. She calls Memphis, TN home and dreams of living close to the ocean... one day.

Also By the Author:

Iced Coffee and Depression: Poetry
Poet Diana Townsend has written a daunting yet relatable collection of poetry that appeals to readers of all ages. Townsend explores her journey with depression, motherhood, her relationships, and her grief and allows readers into her private thoughts. Iced Coffee and Depression is poetry for women who are healing, who are struggling, and/or women who take life one day at a time. Townsend writes in a way where readers can feel welcome to come as they are, hands wrapped around a cup of coffee, and enjoy this beautiful journey of a woman who has been down to the trenches and fought her way back to happiness.

Black Girl Evolving: Poetry
Poet Diana Townsend shares with us a haunting and memorable poetry collection about love, relationships, anxiety, and depression. This is her personal story of growth.

Each poem Townsend writes offers us, as readers, a safe space to cry, reflect, and possibly even heal. She has allowed herself the opportunity to be vulnerable and open with her audience in a way that makes her writing relatable and enjoyable. She is still the same girl from Memphis, TN but she allows us a glimpse into the woman she is becoming and the journey to get there is one we won't soon forget.